2019

Dear Rylan,

Hope you enjoy your trip around the world with the animals! Perhaps one may be entertained by the illustrations now and save narrations for when you are a bit older! Susan, the author, is a friend of mine. Susan's illustration of the Turtle from Turkey. Do you have a favorite?

Love and hugs,
Aunt Susan

To Susan
From Susan
Have a Great Trip!

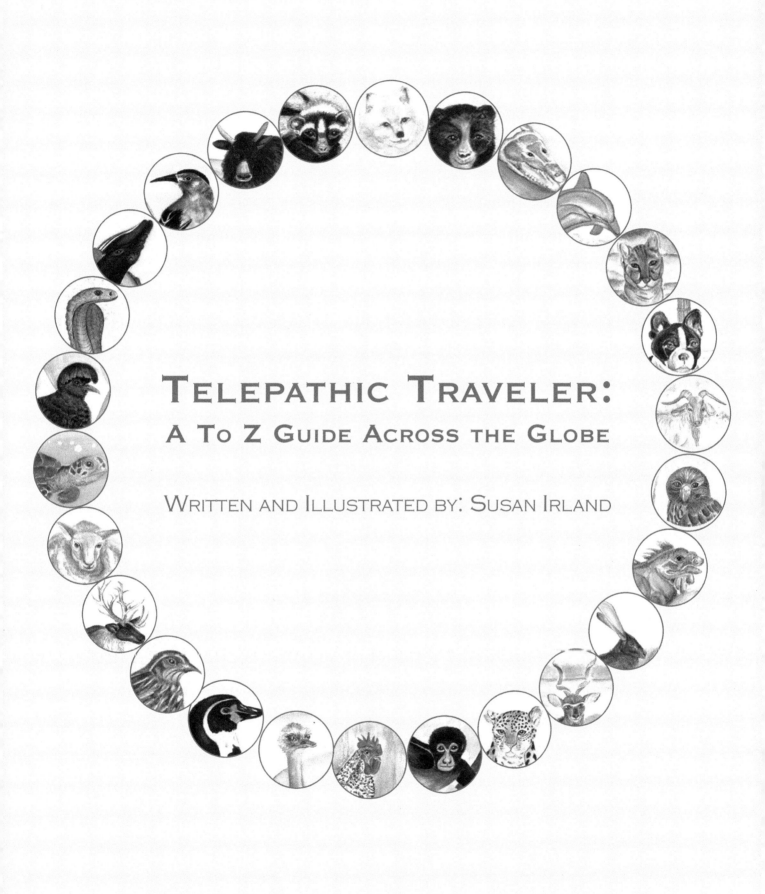

TELEPATHIC TRAVELER:

A To Z Guide Across the Globe

WRITTEN AND ILLUSTRATED BY: SUSAN IRLAND

SHIRES ✺ PRESS
4869 Main Street
P.O. Box 2200
Manchester Center, VT 05255
www.northshire.com

TELEPATHIC TRAVELER:
A To Z Guide Across the Globe

Copyright © 2019 Written and Illustrated by *Susan Irland*

ISBN Number: 978-1-60571-415-8

Building Community, One Book at a Time

*A family-owned, independent bookstore in
Manchester Ctr., VT, since 1976 and Saratoga Springs, NY since 2013.
We are committed to excellence in bookselling.
The Northshire Bookstore's mission is to serve as a resource for
information, ideas, and entertainment while honoring the needs
of customers, staff, and community.*

Printed in the United States of America

CONTENTS

World Map	2-3
Definitions	4-5
The Traveler	6-7
Arctic Fox – United States of America – State of Alaska	8-9
Spectacled Bear – Bolivia	10-11
Crocodile – Costa Rica	12-13
Dolphin – Denmark	14-15
Egyptian Cat – Egypt	16-17
French Bull Dog – France	18-19
Goat – Greece	20-21
Hawk – Haiti	22-23
Iguana – India	24-25
Jack Rabbit – Japan	26-27
Kudu – Kenya	28-29
Leopard – Libya	30-31
Monkey – Mexico	32-33
North Holland Blue Chicken – Netherlands	34-35
Ostrich – Oman	36-37
Penguin – Peru	38-39
Quail – Qatar	40-41
Reindeer – Russia	42-43
Sheep – Sweden	44-45
Turtle – Turkey	46-47
Umbrella Bird – Uruguay	48-49
Viper – Vietnam	50-51
Whale – Wallis Island	52-53
Xinjiang Ground Jay – Xinjiang	54-55
Yak – Yemen	56-57
Zorilla – Zimbabwe	58-59
The Traveler	60-61
Telepathic Traveler Questions	62
References	63-67
Telepathic Traveler Answers	68

Arctic Ocean

Greenland

Baffin Bay

Sweden

Iceland

Norway

Alaska

Canada

Hudson Bay

North America

North Atlantic Ocean

Denmark

U.K.

Netherlands

Ireland
Belgium

Germany
Luxembour
Liechtenstein

United States of America

Europe
France

Andorra

Switzerland

Spain

Monaco Italy
Vatican City

Portugal

Sicily

Morocco

Tunisia

Mexico

Bahamas

Western Sahara

Algeria

Lib

Honduras
Jamaica

Cuba

Haiti

Saint Kitts and Nevis

Mauritania
Senegal

Guatemala

Cha

El Salvador

Belize

Dominican Republic

Banjul

Mali

Niger

Nicaragua

Puerto Rico

Domenica

Gambia

Burkina

Costa Rica

Caribbean Sea

Antigua

Virgin Islands

Guinea
Bissau

Africa

Grenada

Barbados

Ghana

Nigeria

St Lucias

St Vincents and the Grenandines

Sierra Leone

Togo

Panama

Trinidad

Côte D'Ivoire

Benin

Venezuela

Guyana

Tobago

Liberia

Cameroon

Colombia

Ivory Coast

Suriname

Equatirial Guinea

Gabon

Dem Re

South
Pacific Ocean

Ecuador

South America

Sao Tome
Principe

Congo

Peru

Brazil

Angol

Bolivia

South
Atlantic Ocean

Paraguay

Namibia

Chile

Uruguay

Argentina

2

Finland
Estonia

oland Latvia
Lithuania
Belarus
zech Rep.

Russia

North Korea
South Korea

**North
Pacific Ocean**

ustria Hungary
oventia Serbia **Moldova**
lbania Bosnia Montenegro
Croatia Albania Macedonia Turkmenistan
Azerbaijan
maria Cyprus Armenia Iran
Malta Crete **Turkey**
Syria
Jordan
Iraq
Kawait
Egypt **Saudi
Arabia**

Ukraine

Mongolia

Kazakhstan

Uzbekistan Tajikistan
Afghanistan **Xinjiang
Province** **China**
Tibet
Nepal Bhutan
Pakistan
Qatar
Bahrain **India**
United Arab
Emirates

Japan

Taiwan

Philippines

Bangladesh Myanmer
Laos **Asia**
Thailand **Vietnam**

Eritrea
Sudan
entral Djibouti
frican **Ethiopia** **Oman**
epublic **Yemen**
Somalia
Uganda **Kenya**
Rwanda
Burandi

Cambodia

Maldives
Sri Lanka

Brunei Indonesia **Marshall Islands**
Papua New Guinea
Malaysia New Guinea Tuvalu
Singapore Vanuatu
Caroline Islands
Solomon Islands

Tanzania
Comoros **Indian Ocean**
Malawi Seychelles
Zambia
Zimbabwe

Madagascar

otswana Mozambique

Swaziland
Lesotho
outh Africa

Australia

Samoa
Wallis Island
Tonga Islands

New Zealand

Southern Ocean

3

Telepathic tel-e-path-ic *adj* – communication from one mind to another's without speech.

Traveler \tra-vel-er *noun* –
commonly refers to one who travels,
especially to distant lands.

Would you like to be a traveler and visit different animals from around the world?

All right, are you ready?

Let's go…bring your coat, backpack, snow boots, sandals, raincoat, sunglasses, camera and imagination!

You are going to be traveling around our world visiting countries and animals with the different letters in the alphabet!

Aa

Aa
Arctic Fox
United States of America
State of Alaska

"Hello Arctic fox! I notice you're hunting for food. It must be forty degrees below zero. It's sure cold here," the traveler said shivering.

"Yes, I know but I have thick white fur and my feet are furry. This helps to keep me warm in the winter and when I am hunting, my white fur keeps me from being seen. I jump and dig through the snow with my paws to catch my prey," replied Arctic fox.

"Summer is coming soon. In the summer my fur turns brown or gray," said the Arctic fox. "Alaska has a short summer when plants and trees grow and the earth is brown and gray."

"Changing colors is a great way to match the seasons and stay hidden while I am hunting here in Alaska."

"Did you know that Alaska is the largest state in the United States of America? It has glaciers, moose, eagles, and rivers filled with salmon."

"Really, I think I will go and visit some other parts of your state," said the traveler.

"You are a very pretty animal. I'm so glad I got to meet you!"

Bb
Spectacled Bear
Bolivia

"Hola spectacled bear! Why are you basking in the sun in Bolivia?" asked the traveler.

"I love the sunshine. Did you know that I'm the only bear that lives in rugged and steep mountains in South America?" replied the spectacled bear.

"You aren't wearing glasses so why are you called the spectacled bear?" asked the traveler.

"They call us that because some of us are born with white rings around our eyes that look like spectacles."

"Most bears hibernate in the winter, do you?" asked the traveler.

"No, we don't hibernate because the Bolivian climate is not that cold. We build nests in the tops of trees where we eat and sleep. We are small bears and have sharp claws so we can climb trees. We eat leaves, berries and grasses."

"Why are you laughing?" asked the bear.

"Do you know when you talk you sound like a chirping bird? I am going now. I need to get back to my ship," said the traveler.

"I can help you with directions. Go west through Peru to get to the ocean," instructed the spectacled bear.

Cc

Cc
Crocodile
Costa Rica

"Buenos Dias Mr. Crocodile!"

"Good Morning Mr. Crocodile! I'm behind you," said the traveler.

"I know where you are. I can hear and smell really well," answered the crocodile.

"I've just arrived here in Costa Rica. What should I know about your country?"

"Well, it rains a lot here and we have several active volcanoes."

"Did you know people are afraid of you?" asked the traveler.

"We do look like prehistoric creatures and it makes people scared. I would bet people don't know we are scared of them too. All we want to do is swim, catch fish and live in the rivers. People should just live in their villages and we will live along the rivers. Then everything will be perfect," replied the crocodile as he quickly sped away.

"Wow, he is fast! He moves like a snake with his tail going and his legs paddling," the traveler thought to himself.

Dd

Dd
Dolphin
Denmark

"Sikke en hoppe!"

"What a jump!" the traveler yelled from his boat. "You are the first dolphin I've seen in the Baltic Sea. Look at all the islands around Denmark. There are hundreds of them."

The dolphin chimed in, "But, only some of them have people living on them."

"I was awake early this morning, the sun came up at 4:00 a.m.," said the traveler.

"The sun won't set until 10:00 p.m.," replied the dolphin. "We have long summer days but short winter days. In the winter the sun doesn't come up until 9:00 a.m. and it sets at 4:30 p.m."

"It is a delightful day to play," squealed the dolphin. "Diving and leaping makes me go faster. It is our way of running. We can also go faster by riding the wave of a fast moving boat. Let's run! I will ride your wave," said the dolphin.

When it was time for lunch, the dolphin called out several clicks and whistles to his friends. With a big jump and a wave goodbye to the traveler, the dolphin went to find fish for lunch with his friends.

Ee
Egyptian Cat
Egypt

"ءاوم!"

"Meow," the traveler heard as he walked down the path. There, sitting along the desert path, was a wild Egyptian cat. It had a long tail, stripes on his cheeks, yellow gray fur, yellow feet and a short muzzle.

"What a great camouflage," thought the traveler? "If I hadn't heard the ءاوم! meow, I would not have even seen you."

"What are you doing out during the daytime?" the traveler inquired. "Don't you usually hunt and wander about in the evening?"

"Yes, I do," replied the Egyptian cat. "My family is moving down the Nile River. I slept through the night, and now I need to catch up with them. I was just calling to see if they were near by. There they are! I see them down the path," he purred excitedly. "Most of Egypt is desert. Many people and animals live along the Nile River so they will have access to water."

"You'd better run and join them," said the traveler.

"ءاوم! Meow" said the cat as the traveler watched the cat run off to join the family.

Ff
French Bull Dog
France

"Bonjour peu de Bouledogue."

"Good afternoon little bulldog," greeted the traveler. "I have just arrived in Paris. France is a fabulous country and what a beautiful city Paris is!"

"Did you know that more people visit my country than any other country in the world?" replied the French bulldog.

"By the way, I am lost. For a dog bone would you tell me which way to go to find the train station?" said the traveler.

"I understand that your country has 19,784 miles of train tracks and some trains go as fast as 200 miles per hour."

"Go straight ahead," woofed the bulldog.

The traveler gave the dog a bone. "What a friendly dog," thought the traveler.

As the traveler went straight ahead the bulldog shook his head. "What a silly traveler! Didn't he see the sign?"

Gg
Goat
Greece

"Βλέμμα!"

"Look, that man has hair on his chin just like me!" thought the goat. With that, the goat kicked up his heels and bounded over to the man. The traveler stopped to watch the goat and listen.

"Sir, what do they call the hair on your chin?" asked the goat. "It looks great!"

"Why you should know," answered the man giggling.

"It's called a goatee."

"That is funny," mused the goat. "I don't think we look at all alike."

"This is the first time I have had the opportunity to visit with a goat. Tell me about yourself."

"We need bushes, trees and desert scrub and herbs to survive."

"In return, they use us to provide people with milk, meat, and cheese. Can you do that?"

"No," replied the man. "We use your milk, meat, wool and cheese to help us survive."

"We like to climb the mountains. Can you do that?"

"Well, we have a few hikers that climb the mountains, so I guess we could do that."

"I suppose all you really got from us was the goatee," mused the goat.

Hh
Hawk
Haiti

"Bonjou!"

"Good morning! Bonswa," sang the hawk to the traveler. "It is so nice of you to visit the island of Haiti here in the Caribbean. Did you stop and have a cup of our coffee on your way to the forest? One of our main crops is coffee, and it is very good."

The traveler looked and finally spotted the hawk high up in the tree. "Why are you staying so far up in the tree?" asked the traveler.

"From here I can see to hunt for animals," replied the hawk.

"I use my sharp claws, a sharp hooked bill and keen eyes to find my prey. Also, this is where my nest is," replied the hawk.

"I can also see the beautiful ocean and all the lush flowers and trees," sang the hawk.

"Enjoy your stay on the island," the hawk sang as he flew off for a morning flight to hunt for food.

Ii
Iguana
India

" हैलो ट्रैवलर ने इगुआना को भारत में आपका स्वागत किया ! "

"Hello traveler," hissed the iguana. "Welcome to India."

"Hello, I just had an itch on my foot, I looked down and there you were," replied the traveler.

"You came to visit at a good time," said the iguana. "The monsoon season in India will be coming very soon. It is almost June." The iguana started looking around.

"What are you looking for?" asked the traveler.

"I'm looking for spiders and bugs," replied the iguana.

"My brother and I had a fight, and he took my spiders and bugs! I won the fight. That is why I am bright green. That is the color we turn if we win a fight. The loser turns dark yellow. The rest of the time we are gray in the shade or brown when it is very hot or very cold."

"If you want to visit again, wait until September when the monsoon season ends," cautioned the iguana. With that, his tongue came out; he caught a bug, ate it and then crawled away in pursuit of more bugs to eat.

Jj
Jack Rabbit
Japan

"ここで何をする予定ですか。?"

"What are you doing here?" asked the jack rabbit.

"I just wanted to visit Japan, see your islands and visit the famous Mt. Fuji volcano," replied the traveler.

"Mt. Fuji is our highest mountain and is almost perfect in shape. The best way to see it is to go by train," noted the jack rabbit.

The traveler was puzzled. "By the way, jack rabbit, what are you doing here? I thought jack rabbits lived in the southwestern part of the United States."

"You are confused," said the jack rabbit. "A jack rabbit is a male rabbit and a jack rabbit is a breed of rabbit."

"That is a little confusing," said the traveler.

"Not to me," replied the jack rabbit as he jumped up and hopped away.

Kk
Kudu
Kenya

"Umewaona swara wakipita hpa?"

"Have you seen any antelopes go by?" asked the traveler.

"I'm an antelope," called a Kudu. "There are many different antelopes."

"You are a beautiful antelope," said the traveler. "I really like your spiral antlers and stripes. The stripe on your forehead looks like you painted it on."

"What are some of the other animals that live in Kenya?" asked the traveler.

"We have a lot of different wild animals in Kenya. There are animals such as lions, leopards, buffalo, rhinoceros and elephants in our country."

"What is the weather like in your country?"

The kudu continued, "We have a tropical climate on the coast and it is dry in the interior part of the country. This lets you decide which climate you would like to live in. We also have mountains here in Kenya. If you have time you should visit Mount Kenya."

"Well, I had planned to visit Mount Kenya," said the traveler. "I can't wait to see a mountain that is 17,057 feet high!"

Ll
Leopard
Libya

"لقد غادر مدينة طرابلس على ساحل البحر الأبيض المتوسط."

"I just left the city of Tripoli on the coast of the Mediterranean Sea," said the traveler to a fellow passenger sitting on the bus. "Did you know that 90% of Libya is desert? I've been wanting to take a ride into the desert and visit the leopards." Just then, the traveler spotted a leopard cub. "Please stop," he called out to the bus driver. As the bus came to a stop, the traveler leaped off.

"I'm looking for the great athletic leopard," said the traveler to the cub.

"You must be looking for my father," boasted the leopard cub. "He is the largest, leanest and most athletic animal. He can run, swim, climb and jump. When I grow up I want to be just like him," the cub said proudly.

The traveler asked, "Will I be able to meet him?"

"He has gone out hunting in the desert. If you happen to see him tell him his little cub is hungry and he needs to come home soon."

With that, the cub frolicked off!

Mm

Mm
Monkey
Mexico

"Oye allí mono mágico macho from Mexico!"

"Hey there magical macho monkey from Mexico! Please come down from that tree so I can see you and talk to you," called the traveler.

"Okay, but we don't come down on the ground very often; it is a good way to avoid predators. We live in the forests and travel through the tree tops." With that the monkey swung hands to feet, and branch to branch until he reached the ground.

"Boy, I wish I could do that," thought the traveler.

"What kind of monkey are you?" the traveler asked.

"I'm called a spider monkey," he replied.

"Gee, you have two eyes, two ears, two legs, two arms, a nose and teeth. It is kind of strange that you have four fingers and no thumb. You sure don't look like a spider to me," mused the traveler.

The monkey chuckled, "When we hang by our tail we look more like a spider. Having four fingers and no thumb helps us climb. Well, I better get back to the group of monkeys that I live with."

With that, the monkey swung hands to feet, and branch to branch until he reached the top of the tree.

The traveler looked up and in the trees, there must have been forty spider monkeys. "What fun that must be swinging from tree to tree," thought the traveler.

Nn
North Holland Blue Chicken
Netherlands

"Cock-a-doodle-doo aan u."

"Cock-a-doodle-doo to you," crowed the rooster.

"Didn't I see you here last week," inquired the rooster from the Netherlands.

"I didn't know you could remember faces," replied the traveler.

"Where are you going?" asked the rooster.

"I want to visit your famous windmills and see your beautiful tulips," said the traveler.

"Why are you out strutting around?" asked the traveler.

"I'm looking for a place to build a nest for the North Holland Blue hen. When I find the right spot in the straw and grass I will call her to roost."

"How do you make your nest?"

"I sit down and rock back and forth and it forms a nest. While she roosts I will find bugs and grain for her to eat."

"Good luck," said the traveler. "It is interesting that the rooster remembers faces and he cares for the hen. They are smarter than I thought."

Oo

Oo
Ostrich
Oman

"انه على يقين من راح هنا."

"It sure is hot here in Oman," thought the traveler. Just then, he spotted the ostrich. "You are such a big bird," exclaimed the traveler. "I heard you weren't any ordinary bird. But, if I hadn't seen you in person I wouldn't have believed it."

"We are the largest bird," replied the ostrich. "Because we are so big we cannot fly like other birds. Our wings just help us keep our balance when we run. We can run up to 25 to 35 miles per hour. That makes us different than other birds."

"We lay the largest eggs of any bird. During the day our females sit on the eggs and at night the males sit on the eggs."

"We also have thick eyelashes that keep the sand from getting in our eyes. The central part of Oman is sand-covered desert plains. Our long legs and two big toes make it easy to run in the desert."

"Where would you suggest I visit in your country while I am here?" asked the traveler.

"Visit our cities along the coast. They have wonderful beaches for visitors. You can go snorkeling and swimming."

"Thank you for the idea. Swimming will be a great way to cool off after being in the desert," said the traveler.

Pp
Penguin
Peru

"Allí él es!"

"There he is!" Walking down the gangplank from the ship, the traveler wondered what the penguin wanted. Recently, the traveler had received an invitation from the Humboldt penguin to pay a visit to Peru.

"Thank you for coming," said the penguin to the traveler. "I am hoping you can possibly help us. Let me give you a pen and paper so you can write things down."

"Our life in Peru is getting difficult. The fishermen are taking too many fish and we can't get enough to eat. They also are using big nets and we are getting tangled up in them. We can swim 25 miles per hour when we are hunting squid, shrimp and fish to eat. Sometimes we swim right into the nets."

"I've got it written down," said the traveler. "Let's see if we can find another place for the fishermen to fish. If they will go further down the coastline to fish, then you will not get caught in the nets and there will be enough fish for you to eat."

"That would be wonderful." The penguin clapped his flippers and jumped in the water and swam to tell his family. "I think we have found the perfect helper."

Qq

Qq
Quail
Qatar

"كيف تجد لي؟"

"How did you find me?" the surprised quail asked.

"I really didn't find you. I was walking in the grass and came upon you. You really stay well hidden. Your colors match the surrounding fields."

"Don't be frightened, I won't hurt you."

"I am surprised that you are so small. You look about the size of a robin."

"Are you migrating right now?" asked the traveler.

"Yes," answered the quail. "We go north in the spring and south in the winter. Last night we flew about 350 miles at about 37 miles per hour. We are really quick but get very tired when we take these long trips."

"Qatar is a special place for us. This country has sunshine just about every day of the year," said the quail.

With that, the quail lifted his wings and quietly flew low over the fields and disappeared.

Rr

Rr
Reindeer
Russia

"Российские увереииые зимы холодноы!"

"Russian winters sure are cold," the traveler thought as he pulled his hood tighter around his face. Just then he spotted a large reindeer.

"What big antlers you have!" exclaimed the traveler. "You must be a male reindeer if you have antlers."

"No," replied the reindeer. "Both males and females have antlers in the reindeer family. We also have footpads that are sponge-like in the summer for traction and in the winter they shrink so the edge of our hooves will cut into the ice to keep from slipping. It also lets us dig into the snow for moss, our favorite food."

"Are those reindeer swimming in the lake?" questioned the traveler.

"Yes, a reindeer can swim easily and quickly. We will easily swim across a large lake or broad river," the reindeer replied.

"Russia has thousands of rivers and lakes. The largest of Russia's bodies of fresh water is Lake Baikal, the world's deepest, purest, fresh water lake. Lake Baikal alone contains over one fifth of the world's fresh water."

"In northern Russia, the Yamalo-Nenets people breed reindeer to earn a living. They sell the meat to Germany, Italy, Greece and Latvia," noted the reindeer.

When the reindeer had finished talking, he joined the other reindeer swimming across the lake.

Ss

Ss
Sheep
Sweden

"BAA, sa fåren."

"Baa," said the sheep. "I remember when you traveled down this road last summer. I thought you had a kind and gentle face when you stopped to pet me," said the sheep.

"I remember," said the traveler. "It was late in June. Your days in the summer are very long. I was biking on the rolling hills. Daylight lasted eighteen hours."

"Yes, that is true," answered the sheep. "But, in the winter we only have six hours of daylight."

"I didn't recognize you with your thick wooly coat," replied the traveler. "It was sheared off last summer. Your wool coat must keep you very warm in the winter. Having it sheared off in the summer must keep you cool."

"People use our wool to make clothing so they can stay warm in the winter too," replied the sheep. "Just think, your coat may have been made from some of my wool."

Tt
Turtle
Turkey

"Bu baloncuklar sizin," geliyor.

"Are those bubbles coming from you?" asked the turtle.

"They sure are," answered the traveler. "I just had to go snorkeling and swimming in this beautiful Aegean Sea. It is such a magnificent color of blue."

"Turkey is surrounded by three seas. The Aegean Sea is on the western side of our country, the Black Sea is to the northern side of the country and the Mediterranean Sea is in the southern side of the country."

"It is great living here. We can swim all day and go to the beach to lay our eggs. We come back to the same place every year to lay our eggs. It is the perfect spot."

"What is your name?" asked the traveler.

"I am a loggerhead turtle," replied the turtle.

"What do loggerhead turtles eat?" asked the traveler.

"We feed mostly on sponges, worms, snails, clams, squid, octopus, barnacles, horseshoe and other crabs, shrimp, sea urchins, and fish."

"That's funny," mused the traveler. "They eat some of the same things we do."

As the turtle swam away, he called to the traveler "Enjoy your snorkeling and swimming."

Uu

Uu
Umbrella Bird
Uruguay

"El tiempo en Uruguay, sin duda, es diferente a los demás países que hemos visitado," pensó el viajero. Sólo entonces, él heard…

"The weather in Uruguay certainly is different than the other countries we have visited," thought the traveler. Just then, he heard…

"I'm up in the tree," called the long-wattled umbrella bird down to the traveler.

"Why are you sitting so high up?"

"I like to be up high because umbrella birds don't fly that well. Being up high let's me see for miles. That way, I don't have to fly as often."

"It took a long time getting here," said the traveler. "We were hiking for hours. First, it was hot, then it rained, and now it is sunny and bright."

"Our weather changes quite quickly," said the umbrella bird.

"Your landscape is rolling plains. There are no mountains. The weather fronts roll through making it vary from sun to rain in a short amount of time," said the traveler.

All of sudden the traveler exclaimed, "Look at you. What I read is right! They said you had an umbrella on your head and you do."

"It is called a crest," said the umbrella bird. "It keeps the sun and rain out of my eyes."

"Is that where we got the idea for an umbrella? Or did you get your name from our umbrellas?"

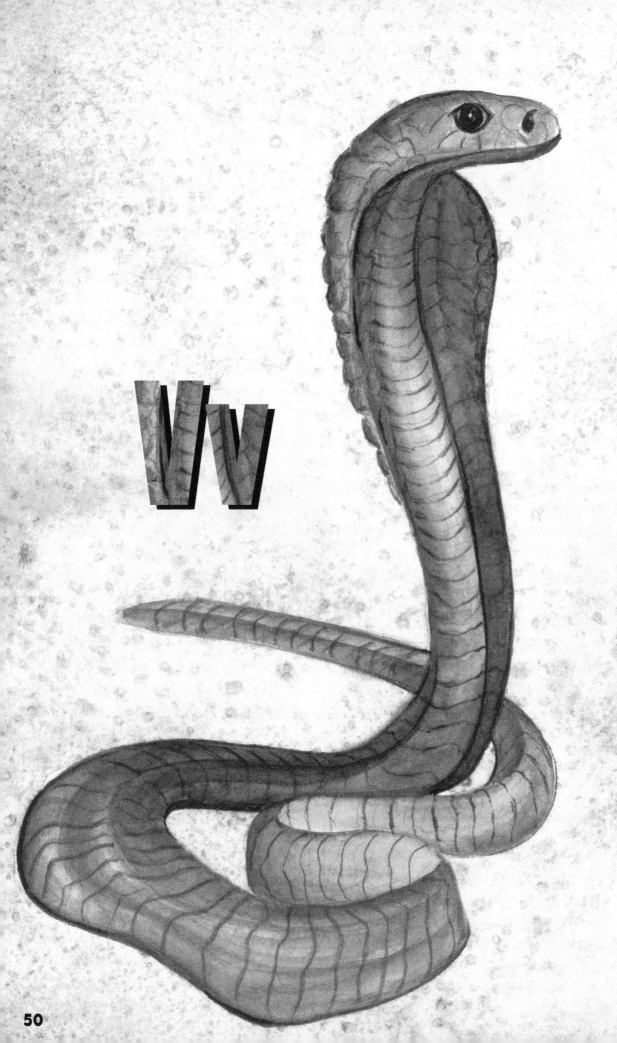

Vv

Vv
Viper
Vietnam

"Làm thế nào để bạn lần lượt, sway và twist?"

"How do you turn, sway and twist?" asked the traveler.

The viper raised himself up to look at the traveler. Not many people had ever stopped to talk to him.

"We have joints that bend," replied the viper. "I am a king cobra and the largest viper. I can grow up to eighteen feet long."

"Tell me more about vipers," said the traveler.

"Vipers have fangs and venom glands. Most people are afraid of vipers. People know that vipers are venomous and don't want to be bitten. Some vipers eat other animals. We help keep the balance of nature by doing that."

"There are over thirty types of vipers in Vietnam. If you live here you have to be careful not to get bitten. Unless cornered, we would rather retreat from people than to bite them."

With that, the viper slithered away leaving the traveler wondering what the viper was going to have for dinner that night.

"I don't think I would like to be a herpetologist," the traveler thought.

Ww

Ww
Whale
Wallis Island

"Il y a l'île de Wallis!"

"There's Wallis Island!" the traveler exclaimed. "It's been a long boat ride from Hawaii to here. The weather is cool and dry. I'm glad it's October. The hot and rainy season doesn't come until November."

The traveler skillfully docked his boat. The course to the dock had been carefully charted to avoid the coral reefs.

Very few tourists visit Wallis Island. It is a small self-governing French territory. Many years ago it was a popular stop for whaling ships.

Just then, the waters of the Pacific Ocean parted and a humpback whale jumped up in the air.

"Wow! What a spectacular sight! That whale must be forty-fifty feet long! It's as long as a big boat! That humpback whale is powerful. What large flippers and what a beautiful tail that whale has. He can see above the water when he is in the air and below the water when he is swimming. I would have to wear goggles and an air tank."

"It was worth coming just to see the humpback whale," thought the traveler.

Xx
Xinjiang Ground Jay
Xinjiang

"新疆傑鳥在哪裡？"

"Where is the Xinjiang Jay bird?" The traveler climbed down the steps from the bus. It had been a long ride from the eastern part of China to the western part of China.

"Here I am," chirped the Xinjiang Jay bird. "We all live here in Xinjiang Province."

"Well, that is an easy way to name a bird," thought the traveler. "I wonder how many places have birds or people with the same names?"

"What does Xinjiang mean?" asked the traveler.

"It means New Frontier," chirped the bird. "Xinjiang covers 617,763 square miles in the western part of China. There is a lot of desert in this part of China."

"Your colors blend in with desert," noted the traveler.

"How do you pronounce your name?"

"shǐn`jyäng," chirped the bird.

"Boy, it's hot here in the summer," exclaimed the traveler.

"It is also very cold here in the winter," chirped the bird. "The best time to visit is in the fall when the days are long and lots of fruits and vegetables are ready to harvest and eat."

The traveler boarded the bus going back to the city. "What a beautiful bird," he thought.

Yy
Yak
Yemen

"هل أنت من ذكر وأ أنثى!"

"Look, there's a big male yak!" exclaimed the traveler as he got off the mountain bike. The traveler leaned his bike up against the fence and walked over to where a yak was grazing.

The traveler had just finished visiting San'a. San'a is one the world's oldest and most beautiful cities. San'a is also the capital of Yemen. Taking the mini bus from the boat to the city was easy. Renting a mountain bike after visiting the city made it possible for the traveler to ride out and see the countryside.

"How did you know I was a male yak?" asked the yak.

"I thought you were a male yak because you have horns," replied the traveler.

"Male and female yaks both have horns. I am a male yak and called a bull. The female yak is called a cow. You might also like to know that we live in herds."

"In Yemen there are many different breeds of yak," he continued. "Farmers raise domesticated yaks and wild yaks roam free. We are very good climbers. Domesticated yaks are kept primarily for their milk, fiber and meat, and are beasts of burden."

"How is your weather here in Yemen?" asked the traveler.

"It can be really hot in the summer. The best time to visit is between November and February. Mid March to mid April we have monsoons."

"Well, Mr. Yak, it has been nice talking with you. I don't have time to yak anymore. It is time to bike back into the city and catch a mini bus back to the boat."

Zz
Zorilla
Zimbabwe

"This is going to be a fun visit," thought the traveler. I like saying "A zorilla from Zimbabwe!"

At that moment the traveler spotted what he thought was a skunk.

"Are you a skunk?" asked the traveler.

"No, I'm a member of the weasel family called a zorilla. We are also referred to as an African polecat or a striped polecat. Zorillas can spray like a skunk. I am black with white bands and spots. That's why sometimes we are mistaken for a skunk. We are both members of the weasel family."

"Why haven't I seen you before?" asked the traveler

"We are nocturnal," replied the zorilla. "At night, we hunt for little animals, birds and bird eggs to eat."

"I am really enjoying my visit to Zimbabwe," said the traveler. "Your country has beautiful wild animals. I have seen zebras, antelopes, giraffes, leopards, lions, rhinos and elephants. I just missed you. I guess you catch your zzzzzz's during the day," the explorer said laughing.

Telepathic Traveler Questions

1. Why is the traveler communicating telepathically? _____

2. Why does the arctic fox change colors? _____

3. Does the spectacled bear hibernate? _____

4. What animal in the book looks prehistoric? _____

5. What country has the longest summer day? _____

6. What is the name of the river that runs down through Egypt? _____

7. Which country in the book has 19,874 miles of train track? _____

8. Which animal supplies milk, meat, and cheese? _____

9. Which country has large crops of coffee beans? _____

10. What color does the iguana turn if it wins a fight? _____

11. What is the highest mountain in Japan? _____

12. Does the Kudu have stripes? _____

13. What can the leopard do? _____

14. Does the spider monkey have a thumb? _____

15. How does the rooster help the Blue Chicken? _____

16. Can the ostrich fly? _____

17. What do the penguins eat? _____

18. What does migrate mean? _____

19. Do male and female reindeer have antlers? _____

20. What is the wool from sheep used for? _____

21. Where do the turtles lay their eggs? _____

22. What is the top of the umbrella bird's head called? _____

23. What is a herpetologist? _____

24. Can the humpback whale jump? _____

25. Is Xinjiang a country or a province? _____

26. What is a male yak called? _____

27. The zorilla is part of what family of animals? _____

62

(see answers pg 69)

REFERENCES

ARCTIC FOX-ALASKA

The New Larousse Encyclopedia of Animal Life, Bonanza Books-New York, ©Paul Hamlyn Limited l967

http://animals.nationalgeographic.com/animals/mammals/arctic-fox.html

http://en.wikipedia.org/wiki/Artic

The Handy Geography Answer Book, Second Edition -Your Smart Reference, Paul A. Tucci and Matthew T Rosenberg, Visible Ink Press-©2009

SPECTACLED BEAR-BOLIVIA

http://encarta.msn.com/encyclopedia_761579752/spectacled_bear.html

http://www.bears.org/animals/spectacled/

http://www.cecalc.ula.ve/BIONINFORMATICA/oso/spectacled_bear_cont.htm

CROCODILE-COSTA RICA

http://animals.nationalgeographic.com/animals/reptiles/american-crocodile.html

http://jrscience.wcp.muohio.edu/fieldcourses03/PapersCostaRicaArticles/CrocilesinCosta

The New Larousse Encyclopedia of Animal Life, Bonanza Books-New York, ©Paul Hamlyn Limited l967

The Handy Geography Answer Book, Second Edition -Your Smart Reference, Paul A. Tucci and Matthew T. Rosenberg, Visible Ink Press-©2009

DOLPHIN-DENMARK

The New Larousse Encyclopedia of Animal Life, Bonanza Books-New York, ©Paul Hamlyn Limited l967

The Handy Geography Answer Book, Second Edition -Your Smart Reference, Paul A. Tucci and Matthew T Rosenberg, Visible Ink Press-©2009

http://animals.nationalgeographic.com/animals/mammals/bottlenose-dolphin.html

http://en.wikipedia.org/wiki/Dolphin#Jumping_and_playing

EGYPTIAN CAT-EGYPT

A Field Guide to the Mammals of Egypt, Richard Hoath, 2003, The American University in Cairo Press ISBN 977 424 809 0

Natural Selections-A Year of Egypt's Wildlife, Richard hoath, 1992, The American University in Cairo Press ISBN 977-424-281-5

http://www.touregypt.net/featurestories/cats.htm

FRENCH BULL DOG-FRANCE

http://en.wikipedia.org/wiki/Transport_in_France

http://www.factsaboutfrance.net/

The Handy Geography Answer Book, Second Edition-Your Smart Reference, Paul A. Tucci and Matthew T Rosenberg, Visible Ink Press-©2009

GOAT-GREECE

http://ressources.ciheam.org/om/pdf/c05/95605261.pdf

http://capra.iespana.es/capra/ingles/internacional/grecia/greece.htm

HAWK-HAITI

https://www.cia.gov/library/publications/the-world-factbook/geos/ha.html

http://encarta.msn.com/encyclopedia_761576153_4/haiti.htm

IGUANA-INDIA

http://encarta.msn.com/encyclopedia_761557562_2/India.html#p31

The New Larousse Encyclopedia of Animal Life, Bonanza Books-New York, ©Paul Hamlyn Limited 1967-p305

The Handy Geography Answer Book, Second Edition -Your Smart Reference, Paul A. Tucci and Matthew T Rosenberg, Visible Ink Press-©2009

JACK RABBIT-JAPAN

The New Larousse Encyclopedia of Animal Life, Bonanza Books-New York, ©Paul Hamlyn Limited 1967-p519

The Handy Geography Answer Book, Second Edition -Your Smart Reference, Paul A. Tucci and Matthew T Rosenberg, Visible Ink Press-©2009

KUDU-KENYA
The New Larousse Encyclopedia of Animal Life, Bonanza Books-New York,©Paul Hamlyn Limited l967

The Handy Geography Answer Book, Second Edition -Your Smart Reference, Paul A. Tucci and Matthew T Rosenberg, Visible Ink Press-©2009

LEOPARD-LIBYA
The New Larousse Encyclopedia of Animal Life, Bonanza Books-New York, ©Paul Hamlyn Limited l967-p305

The Handy Geography Answer Book, Second Edition -Your Smart Reference, Paul A. Tucci and Matthew T Rosenberg, Visible Ink Press-©2009

MONKEY-MEXICO
The New Larousse Encyclopedia of Animal Life, Bonanza Books-New York, ©Paul Hamlyn Limited l967, p505-506

http://encarta.msn.com/encyclopedia_761565356/Spider_Monkey.html

NORTH HOLLAND BLUE CHICKEN-NETHERLANDS
The Inner World of Farm Animals, Steward, Tabori & Chang, New York-HNA (Harry N.Abrams, Inc., 115 West 18th St, NY, NY, ©2009
Amy Hatkoff

OSTRICH-OMAN
The New Larousse Encyclopedia of Animal Life, Bonanza Books-New York, ©Paul Hamlyn Limited l967

The Handy Geography Answer Book, Second Edition-Your Smart Reference, Paul A. Tucci and Matthew T Rosenberg, Visible Ink Press-©2009

PENGUIN-PERU
http://www.encyclopedia.com/topic/penguin.aspx

http://www.penguins.cl/penguins/humboldt-penguins.jpg

QUAIL-QATAR
The New Larousse Encyclopedia of Animal Life, Bonanza Books-New York, ©Paul Hamlyn Limited l967

The Handy Geography Answer Book, Second Edition -Your Smart Reference, Paul A. Tucci and Matthew T Rosenberg, Visible Ink Press-©

REINDEER-RUSSIA

http://www.answers.com/topic/reindeer

The New Larousse Encyclopedia of Animal Life, Bonanza Books-New York, ©Paul Hamlyn Limited l967

The Handy Geography Answer Book, Second Edition -Your Smart Reference, Paul A. Tucci and Matthew T Rosenberg, Visible Ink Press-©2009

SHEEP-SWEDEN

The New Larousse Encyclopedia of Animal Life, Bonanza Books-New York, ©Paul Hamlyn, Limited l967

The Handy Geography Answer Book, Second Edition -Your Smart Reference, Paul A. Tucci and Matthew T Rosenberg, Visible Ink Press-©2009

The Inner World of Farm Animals, Steward, Tabori & Chang, New York-HNA (Harry N.Abrams, Inc., 115 West 18th St, NY, NY, ©2009 Amy Hatkoff

TURTLE-TURKEY

http://www.cccturtle.org/sea-turtle-information.php?page=loggerhead

http://marinebio.org/species.asp?id=163

http://encarta.msn.com/encyclopedia_761582459/Ecosystem.html#p14

The New Larousse Encyclopedia of Animal Life, Bonanza Books-New York, ©Paul Hamlyn Limited l967

The Handy Geography Answer Book, Second Edition -Your Smart Reference, Paul A. Tucci and Matthew T Rosenberg, Visible Ink Press-©2009

Bonanza Books-New York   Copyright Paul Hamlyn Limited l967

UMBRELLA BIRD-URUGUAY

http://www.cccturtle.org/sea-turtle-information.php?page=loggerhead

http://marinebio.org/species.asp?id=163

http://encarta.msn.com/encyclopedia_761582459/Ecosystem.html#p14

The New Larousse Encyclopedia of Animal Life, Bonanza Books-New York, ©Paul Hamlyn Limited l967

The Handy Geography Answer Book, Second Edition -Your Smart Reference, Paul A. Tucci and Matthew T Rosenberg, Visible Ink Press-©2009

VIPER-VIETNAM

http://animals.nationalgeographic.com/animals/reptiles/king-cobra.html

http://www.reptileknowledge.com/squamat/king-cobra-snake.php

Step Into Reading, S-S-Snakes! By Lucille Recht Penner- Text ©1994, Random House Children's Books

The New Larousse Encyclopedia of Animal Life, Bonanza Books-New York, ©Paul Hamlyn Limited l967

WHALE-WALLIS ISLAND

http://www.acsonline.org/factpack/humpback.htm

http://www.lonelyplanet.com/wallis-and-futuna/history

http://www.mahina.com/5c97-11.html

http://www.britanica.com/Ebchecked/topic/634937/Wallis-and-Futuna

XINJIANG GROUND JAY-XINJIANG PROVINCE

http://www.travelchinaguide.com/cityguides/xinjiang/

http://encyclopedia2.thefreedictionary.com/Xinjiang+province

YAK-YEMEN

The New Larousse Encyclopedia of Animal Life, Bonanza Books-New York, ©Paul Hamlyn Limited l967

The Handy Geography Answer Book, Second Edition -Your Smart Reference, Paul A. Tucci and Matthew T Rosenberg, Visible Ink Press-©2009

ZORILLA-ZIMBABWE

http://images.google.com/imgres?imgurl=http://itech.pic.edu/sctag/zorilla/zorillakill.jpg&im...

http://www.2cit.cornell.edu/services/cubs/vocabulary.html

Telepathic Traveler Answers

1. Because the animals can't talk
2. To protect from predators
3. No, the climate is too warm
4. Crocodile
5. Denmark
6. Nile
7. Paris
8. Goat
9. Haiti
10. Green
11. Mt. Fuji
12. Yes
13. Run, swim, climb and jump
14. No
15. He makes the nest
16. No
17. Fish
18. Moving north to south depending on the climate
19. Yes
20. To make clothing
21. On the beach
22. Crest
23. Someone who studies reptiles like snakes
24. Yes
25. Province
26. Bull
27. Weasel

About the Author and Illustrator

Susan Irland uses her original artwork and a fun storyline to encourage children to use critical skills while taking a whirlwind tour of the world.

Susan spent her childhood in upstate New York and currently resides in New Jersey. She has won awards for her paintings and has taught fine art and illustration both in the public school system and as an adjunct on a college level. One assignment that students were quite frequently given was to illustrate the written word. As a result, the inspiration came to write and illustrate *Telepathic Traveler*. Susan has a bachelor of science in studio and art history and a master's degree in supervision and administration with a visual arts focus. In addition, she has successfully completed numerous fine art graduate level courses at several colleges. She devotes her time to painting, working with students, exploring all the arts, travel (loves the Jersey Shore, Vermont and Maine and the cultural experiences in New York City) and spending time with family and friends.